PENGUIN ANANDA

DANCING WITH SWANS

A devotee of Sai Baba of Shirdi, Ruzbeh N. Bharucha is one of the most influential spiritual writers of our times. He is the author of eighteen books, including the bestselling Fakir trilogy, which has been translated into several languages. In 2014, *Rabda: My Sai . . . My Sigh*, published by Penguin Books, was an instant bestseller.

A former journalist, Ruzbeh is also a documentary film-maker. His documentary *Sehat . . . Wings of Freedom*, on AIDS and HIV in Tihar Jail, was screened at the XVII International AIDS Conference in 2008. His collaboration with Zambhala—India's yoga, music and life spirit festival, the first of its kind—gave birth to a series of powerful videos called 'Ramblings with Ruzbeh Bharucha'. His articles have been published in the *Times of India*, *Free Press Journal*, *Indian Express*, *Maharashtra Herald*, *Sunday Observer*, *Jam-e-Jamshed* and *Afternoon*. His book *My God Is a Juvenile Delinquent* has been included in the reading list of all judicial academies in India. Ruzbeh is the 110th Master for the 'Speaking Tree', where he writes an immensely popular blog on spirituality.

His Facebook page has reached out to thousands in a very short span of time. The daily affirmations and messages are a source of inspiration to many. He lives with his family in Pune.

You can reach him here:
Facebook: www.facebook.com/ruzbehbharucha
Twitter: @ruzbehnbharucha
Website: www.ruzbehbharucha.net
YouTube: www.youtube.com/channel/UCo-rFxiF7R9qaMMWdpj5fJQ

Dancing with
Swans

· A Book of Quotes ·

Ruzbeh N. Bharucha

A Powerful Tool for Constant Guidance and Grace.
An Awakening.

PENGUIN
ANANDA

An imprint of Penguin Random House

PENGUIN ANANDA

USA | Canada | UK | Ireland | Australia
New Zealand | India | South Africa | China

Penguin Ananda is part of the Penguin Random House group of companies
whose addresses can be found at global.penguinrandomhouse.com

Published by Penguin Random House India Pvt. Ltd
7th Floor, Infinity Tower C, DLF Cyber City,
Gurgaon 122 002, Haryana, India

First published in Penguin Ananda by Penguin Random House India 2018

10 9 8 7 6 5 4 3 2 1

ISBN 9780143443094

Typeset in Adobe Caslon Pro by Manipal Digital Systems, Manipal
Printed at Manipal Technologies Limited, Manipal

www.penguin.co.in

On the hundredth year of Baba Sai of Shirdi taking Maha Samadhi, I would like to dedicate this work on behalf of all of us who love our Baba and try our level best to make Him happy and proud.

I have been told You left Your physical body hundred years ago. I say, what nonsense! You live in the hearts, minds, breaths and sighs of countless of Your followers and lovers. So, how could You ever leave Your body as everything of ours is Yours and if all of ours is Yours, then You reside in millions of us, whether we occupy the physical plane or whichever dimension we are meant to be in.

You, my dear Master, the Fakir of Shirdi; You, The One in whom reside The Goddess and The Lord and the Oneness Family; You, the Emperor of our very being and the ruler of our destiny—on behalf of all your lovers, from the past, present, future and beyond the beyond, I dedicate this humble offering to Thou.

Contents

Introduction

It was this time last year when I was guided to sit for meditation after sunset for a certain number of weeks. Thus, every evening, I would sit in my Temple and meditate. After what seemed like an hour, when in reality it was less than ten minutes, I would begin to get these quotes floating about in the bylanes of my blank mind. I would tell Baba Sai, 'If You don't mind, I need to write down these quotes,' and then scribble a quote and pretend to meditate till another quote came about and thus for an hour this song and dance continued. In those weeks, each evening, I would write these quotes down and for a minute or two meditate. Often, I would just tell Baba that, 'Today, I shall lie down in the corpse pose and meditate', only to realize after half an hour that I was snoring my lungs out, which I would tell Baba, 'Very deep meditation, Baba, along with intense and loud pranayama.'

This book is a compilation of those quotes. I must have written about five hundred of them in those weeks.

The theme of this book, in reality, is very simple. Give your best to each moment and leave the rest to The One and after that accept your lot with joyous acceptance. Be kind. Be compassionate. Be a bit crazy. Try not to be an adult. Be childlike and not childish. Be mature, not cynical. Don't judge. Live and let live. Spend time in work, prayer and play. We are the makers of our own destiny through the use of free will in our past lives, this one and the future. Destiny might not change but the little free will we have can decide how we go through our destiny. When life is rubbing our noses into the ground, inhale the fragrance of Mother Earth. When life is tossing us in the air, try and gaze into the sky. All is as well as we want it to be. All is as damned as we would make it out to be. We shall leave this physical body, and we should make sure that we made the world a slightly better place than we found it. This is our little world with our little ability to pass forth light and laughter. Always have faith in the Divine Wisdom, Love and Compassion. *Sab theek hain. Fikar Not.*

Be blessed always.

Jai Baba! Jai Maa! Jai Oneness Family!

Dancing with
Swans

I

Prayer

Pray as though it is the last time we shall get the opportunity and that it shall be our last prayer, and also pray as though the life of our loved ones depends on our prayers.

No matter what, when we reach a place of true acceptance, unconditional acceptance that S(H)E knows best, it is then that true, permanent growth takes place—spiritual, emotional, mental, physical. This is where prayer and faith is meant to take us.

Even if a person spends time alone, on and off, chanting
The Name, drop by drop the ocean will fill.

Prayers that have come from a heart filled with gratitude and love, play the role of a serene oasis for a traveller walking through the desert and hot sands of the laws of give and take, to take rest and be comforted.

The purpose of prayer is to become one with The One.
To seek forgiveness. To ask for mercy. To offer thanks.
To yearn to move away from duality to Oneness, to move
away from darkness into light.

The best way to pray is when you truly send yourself to
The One who you are praying to or pull The One you are
praying to, to come and sit in front of you. Either your
love and thoughts travel to The One where you can see
Him or Her or The Energy in your mind's eye, or you can
feel Him or Her or The Energy sitting or standing a few
feet away from you, hearing you, sensing your love, feeling
your yearning.

~❦~

There needs to be power for anything to defy gravity. Our prayers, if not fuelled with pure, innocent love and gratitude and yearning, will not have the velocity to break through, and go beyond the beyond.

~❦~

Try to purify your soul with prayers and more prayers, good deeds and more good deeds, till you cannot do any more. This is purification of your soul which will form a pond of still water and the lotus that grows in this purified pond will be your last incarnation after which you will merge with God.

You may pronounce the words immaculately, but if the words aren't coming from the very breath of your essence, the very sigh of your soul, then those prayers might as well be verbalized by an intelligent parrot.

You need no pilgrimages. No paraphernalia. No pujari. No flame. No fruits. No flowers. Nothing. You are the devotee. You are the one praying to The One within you. So you are praying and being prayed to. You are the one chanting and being chanted to. You are The One.

All our prayers, chanting and meditation become completely devoid of the true Divine Presence if we are filled with anger and hate, and play the victim and we cannot live to spread our Creator's joy and radiance within and around us.

Often, sadness or emptiness within is a reflection of the yearning of the soul to move towards The One. Those who understand this, move into silence and prayer, or spread joy and compassion. That's the only antidote to fill the void within.

When we pray for forgiveness and our plea reaches the higher self of all those whom we have hurt, slowly the anger which resides in the aura of those individuals begins to fade away, and forgiveness comes forth from the higher self, and the bond of anger and hate and slander vanishes, leading to a peaceful bond or conclusion.

II

Spirituality and Faith

Spiritual pursuit is not an act. It is one's very reason for existence. Something one doesn't just do, but one lives for and eventually becomes. It is not something to be over with, but it is a state we should be in each waking moment of our lives.

❦

Every soul is sacred, the *atma* being a part of the *parmatma*, only the level of enlightenment and realization varies.

❦

The emptiness the seeker feels on The Path is a must. One needs to be empty for the Divine Energy to fill us up. The page has to be blank for the Divine Words to be written on.

Faith means living with the awareness that S(H)E knows best. It is to be nurtured in the soul with the light from one's eternal spirit.

Surrender is a strong word. For anything external and of the world, it means accepting defeat. When one does so to The One, it means divine and eternal victory.

When on The Path, the danger lies in what we choose: *siddhi*, meaning power, or *shudhi*, meaning purity. The first choice without the latter may take us away from The Path. The other will, for certain, make us The Path.

No matter how heavy the cross may be during the walk on The Path homewards, there is nothing heavier than our higher self carrying the cross mired with reactions, compulsions and/or stagnation.

I doubt if S(H)E wants our prayers and offerings, and all
the usual song and dance we indulge in Their name.
S(H)E wants our joyful acceptance of whatever S(H)E
has in store for us. That bond is eternal. That bond has
the fragrance of true love.

The softest of whisper said with a selfless heart, reaches the Perfect Master instantly. All other communication has to pass various filtering channels of karma, planets and intent.

Spirituality means, to operate from the spirit. If you operate from the spirit, you operate from Oneness, and if you operate from Oneness, you can never go wrong.

The only aim in life for every living organism is to merge and realize his or her true origin and become one with The Fakir. This is and should be the only true priority of every individual. All other priorities are clouded with maya, or illusion, and wants and desires and duality; only yearning to realize Oneness is the sole and true priority of each individual.

In spirituality, what one does is far more important than what one can do, or what one wants to do. Walking The Path takes us home. Nothing else will.

It's all about one's priority. If the sole priority is to be always in connection and filled with The One, then our entire attitude towards life and its innumerous ups and downs will not shake us out of our core centredness. It's as simple as that or as impossible.

If you want attention, fame, importance, go ahead and make a song and dance about it. But if you want to surrender to The Master, do it so silently that even you are not aware of it.

Spirituality means Oneness and when you operate from the spirit, never forgetting that eventually only Oneness is true and everything that creates shadows and duality are false, then I would like to believe that the individual has begun the walk on the spiritual path.

If you have to compromise yourself with one role, then let that role be the spark from The Great Flame. Let the role be the dust beneath your Master's fancy feet. That makes so much music. So much sense. So much justification. All other roles are transitory.

Walk the middle path—Dharma, Karma and Yagna. Balance yourself. Pace yourself. You could appear a *bhogi*, but what's most important is to be a yogi within your deepest consciousness.

Not the path of religion but that of spirituality comes from loving God.

Till one does not make God, Goddess, Guru—the 3Gs—as the sole and soul priority, there are innumerable distractions, obstacles, temptations, confusions, to make life a living hell, this and in future lives.

One needs to be filled with light to spread light. From darkness, only darkness can come forth. Only light can spread its radiance.

All religions put together are not worth the life of an
innocent person, for in that innocent person resides
God, and nothing can weigh heavier than the living
God in all beings.

The purpose of life is to go beyond the demands of the transitory and merge with the radiance of permanence.

The tiniest of the burning flame has still the power to vanquish darkness. The minutest of faith has the power to vanquish the darkness of the spirit.

There is a difference of heaven and hell in being prepared for something going wrong and worrying about something going wrong; giving one's best and hoping for the best; living spiritual and being spiritual.

Either become Their dust or merge with The One.
Everything else in between is a waste of life.

When you live with the awareness that the very next moment you or your loved ones could leave the body, then living in a state of gratitude, humility and compassion, as well as appreciation and humour, becomes a way of life.

No matter how ignoble, flawed or damaged we may be, we have come forth from The One and no mother ever forsakes her child, no matter how lost he or she may be. Thus, it is never ever too late to begin the long walk back home. S(H)E never keeps the door locked. Always a light is burning within.

If prayers, meditation, charity and becoming mediums for the Oneness Family do not make us better human beings, then we are going very wrong somewhere. The more filled with ego we are, the less we are on the path of spirituality. Being spiritual starts with living as Their dust.

III

The Guru

The Guru is like a mother, all merciful and with a heart that beats and bleeds for the disciple.

The Guru doesn't want us to move towards
the light, S(H)E wants us to become the light.
When we go astray, The Master hurts. When we get
cleansed, The Master suffers with us. When we go off The
Path, The Master awaits patiently for the child to return.

Loving The Master is the easy path.
Living The Master is the real path.

The Master's role in the life of a devotee or a disciple is not to change and manipulate the karmic blueprint; the role of The Master is to help each child go through their lot and their karma and the experiences with calmness, wisdom, courage and positive acceptance. That is the true role of The Master.

IV

Conduct

The purpose of inherent tendencies is to pull us down, but the inherent nature of the spirit is to soar. The more the focus on the Divine Spirit, the more our spirit will gravitate towards The One. The more the focus on the external, the more we shall be pulled down.

Indulging in slander is like digging an endless pit by oneself which negates all good. It is a slow poison being released into our own land. It makes the land barren and, after a point, a nestling place for scavengers and, eventually, a dump yard for sewage.

Do not oscillate between faith and fear. Don't give
the dark energy more power. Trust Their wisdom and
foresight. Truly believe and hold on to the fact that
S(H)E knows best. Keep the gloves on.

A smile, a kind word, a helping hand and tenderness mean much more for somebody down and out than all the wisdom of all the scriptures put together.

Sometimes, those who are full of themselves seem to be very detached from one and all. That's not detachment; that's proof of self-centredness. The ego that we talk about is not about pride, but it's about self-importance. Pride is often needed to soar, but self-importance is nothing but sinking sand.

What we seek for ourselves, sometimes, comes forth from not knowing our true selves and needs and priorities, thus even after getting what we desire, the void only seems to get wider and deeper.

When somebody takes advantage of your goodness and you are aware of it, and still allow yourself to be used, then you have not only let yourself down, but also all those who have sacrificed themselves for walking The Path.

When you are in control of your mind, then you are in control of your life, your emotions, your sanity and your harmony. But when your thoughts rule you, you are like a slave in your own house.

When thoughts assail us and we try to fight or indulge them, we give the thought more power and karma. Focus on the moment or the name. That will weaken the might of unwanted thoughts.

Guilt and fear cripple the soul. Anger and jealousy burn
the heart. Slander and manipulation pollute the mind.
We know all this and still never let go. For some reason,
mankind is still considered the most intelligent species.

Lust isn't limited to sex. A man desperate for spiritual powers, or blinded by money or fame or even respect, are all gasping in the bowels of lust.

Silence when calm can bring the very Gods to the chambers of your heart and your surroundings, but silent anger attracts lower energies to the person, as it initially creates tiny spots and then holes in the aura and distorts the vibrations in the surroundings.

When you have been going through life in a stagnant haze, where for lifetimes you have been caught in a web of boredom, sloth, anger, greed, lust, listlessness, slander, jealousy, that means you have not been growing; it makes the very heavens weep.

Our problems arise because instead of prostrating ourselves in front of The One, we have prostrated ourselves to our own mind. Either it will serve us or enslave us.

Ironically, the only way one can go beyond one's inherent negative tendency is by not surrendering to its pull and destructive power. Take note. It eventually all comes down to what one is surrendering to.

Never underestimate the power of one's ego and self-destructiveness. Always remember that there is no mantra created that can cure stupidity.

Oscillation of mood and faith is the worst possible impediment to peace and sanity as well as to spiritual consistency and growth. Life becomes akin to a beautiful meadow with innumerable landmines.

So many of us fast, some let go of alcohol, some cigarettes, and some meat, in the name of The One. Very few of us give up our inherent internal weaknesses in the name of The One. Imagine forty days fasting the self of ego, anger, slander, jealousy, envy and negative thoughts. Then we would truly be doing *upwhas*, meaning residing with the higher self.

I am sure even weeds have their own fragrance. That doesn't mean one allows the land to be ravaged by them. Emotions and senses aren't the best GPS system to reach one's destination.

To slander, gossip, and do verbal postmortem about a man who has passed away is like vultures relishing a carcass.

What one sees need not be the truth. I see the sunrise when in reality we all know it's the earth serenading the sun. Ignorance is the worst of all evils.

Not many of us would like to be near somebody who is filled with sewage or has an illness which can be passed on. Yet we carry within us the filthiest of emotions, thoughts, desires, and nurture jealousy, anger, hate and envy.

When religion and spirituality, education and literacy,
knowledge and wisdom, being aware and being realized
mean the same thing in spirit, the very heavens will envy
mankind. Until then, one will not need to
die to experience hell.

In the name of love, there has been more sorrow created. In the name of faith, more doubt. In the name of God, more hate. Mankind has the potential to be Gods or the scum of creation.

Living without knowing one's true strengths, weaknesses and limitations is like driving a beast of a vehicle with eyes shut and hands off the steering wheel.

The instinct of survival is one of the greatest excuses and reasons for the dark path to thrive. Sometimes, the instinct of survival is nothing but self-centredness.

No matter what you do, all the logical explanations and counselling you dish out; guiding and goading and being a sounding board; pilgrimages and spiritual practices; getting to meet spiritual people and so-called psychics and mediums—nothing is going to work till one decides that enough is enough, I have to get my life on track, no more self-destructive activities or playing the victim.

If the intellect is scattered and the individual is not aware of his or her priority—and being unaware of one's priority is like travelling without knowing the destination, the journey's route, the travel conditions, the weather conditions, the places of halt—the journey can become very chaotic and exceedingly cumbersome.

Why do we do the things we do, like slander and playing the victim, knowing very well that we are spreading sadness and negativity and anger and hate and tears like a stench, and yet, why do we still do it? God alone knows what this does to our karmic blueprint. Yes, God, Goddess, Guru, will always still be with us, but what a sad place to make them reside. In a shell, which breeds slander and is perpetually playing the victim.

Often, reality is in front of us but we just put our heads in the sand. Two plus two will always remain four. In every language. In every civilization. In every dimension.

Power that leads to compassion and humility has the fragrance of divinity. If it leads to pride, it is like a rose garden flooded with sewage water.

All that is spiritual leads us to Oneness. Earlier, being religious and spiritual meant the same. Now nothing divides one brother from another as surely as the false interpretation of religion.

Every woman has the Goddess energy active within her.
If channelled well, she creates heaven. If not, she burns
all in her path, including herself.

Why should we be concerned about how creation began?
Instead, we should be truly worried about how we are
hastening its end by our egos.

Don't waste time on negative stuff. Don't. In a blink of a
moment, we shall be either old, alone or dead, and then
realize what we have let slip away from our grasp. All this
shit isn't worth it. Let it go.

It's always a difficult task to show somebody the light, somebody who refuses to remove the thick band they have wrapped their eyes with. The cloak of denial is made of the darkest shade of black known to creation.

When you stop reacting to situations emotionally but react in a positive, silent manner and not in a defeatist or angry-silent manner, then an individual has achieved the silence of the heart. Immediately, you will stop judging people.

Don't let bitterness cloud our soul, our higher self and spiritual potential. Most importantly, let us not make our bitterness make our Master feel despondent and defeated.

We can stand by the window all through the night; the sun will rise at its appointed hour. One can spend the night in agitation and make a nuisance of oneself or we can make good the time and welcome the new day with a smile.

We are all beggars. Each one of us. We are always in want of something. Remember this when someone asks something of us. We are all in the same boat. Money, desire, children, health, love . . . Always in want.

When we judge somebody, it means we are aware of all the facts and thus judge. But most actions could in reality be just reactions due to what started in our past lifetimes. How do we truly know the why–how–when–who of any situation or conduct? Thus, it's stupid to judge.

We are at the mercy of fanatics, plunderers and ruthless leaders. Not because they are powerful but because we are silent and on our own individual survival mode, and in this life or the next we will pay a high price for our silence.

Sometimes, tiredness and a void creep into the very soul. Best to surround oneself with innocence, wisdom or joy, be it in a human being, an animal or art. It helps.

Don't waste your energy trying to prove somebody wrong,
but always stand up for what you truly believe is right.

V

Wisdom

The body may thirst for wine, but one may truly need water. The wise know the difference between their wants and their needs.

Oscillation in our spiritual pursuits very often comes about when we operate from overt eagerness, or bite more than we can chew. This happens when we are not truly aware of our strengths, weaknesses and limitations.

Sometimes, what a chocolate can do for the state of mind and well-being, the scriptures can't. Feel the pulse of the moment. That is spiritual common sense.

A wrong doesn't become right by raising one's voice or by being aggressive. In fact, right becomes wrong if expressed to hurt or wound somebody.

The more one chases something, the farther it usually moves away. The very word 'chase' means to run after something. Don't chase, give your best and just be.

Anybody with common sense knows that fame and popularity are not friends, just loud neighbours one can't do much about.

Do unto others what you would want others to do to you is a good philosophy. It is one of the most underrated spiritual gems of all times.

When we die, will it matter what people say about us?
Then, why should it matter now, what they say,
when we live?

Dust to dust is a reality most people know about but very few truly understand, and fewer live.

Don't let gut feelings lead our lives. There is no substitute for common sense and calm reflection. Leave the gut for digestion.

If we have to convince others of an action or decision, it's understandable, but if we have to vehemently justify to ourselves about something, then it's best to pause and truly think things over.

Every single moment, we either create a dream or a nightmare, as each moment we either choose to live or choose to kill the opportunity to live.

The highs and lows of life seem a distant memory. All that remains is the manner in which one embraced or resisted the moment.

We would call somebody an idiot if we saw him trying to clench water in a fist rather than cupping it gently in the palms. And yet, we go about doing the same when it comes to accepting what life has in store for us.

Don't seek validation from the world. It has a tendency to crucify whoever it once loved.

The flame cleanses the sage and the sinner.
Never judging, never questioning. Always spreading
the radiance, hoping someday we get out of darkness
and spread light unconditionally.

We all are vessels. What we decide to fill ourselves up with will decide eventually where we will be used. In reality, all scriptures are about this simple reality. The pot that carries the Ganges water will be taken to the temple. The pot that carries dirty water will reach someplace else.

Our temperament is our barometer of peace and chaos within, or of heaven and hell. It's how we accept internally what life dishes out to us. It's not about life; it's about how we accept it.

The way forward sometimes begins by clearing the backlog left behind. Sometimes, one needs to take a step back in order to leap ahead.

Often, the freshness of the fruit depends on knowing when to pluck it, how to keep it and when to eat it. Same as one's quality of life. When to speak, how to speak and when to shut up.

A gallon of vinegar isn't needed when a spoonful of sugar can do the work. By being watchful of our words, we save ourselves from the grief and headache caused by the futility of reaction.

Eventually, every drop is going to decide the quality of the goblet of water that you and I offer to The One. How much ever you take care of the milk, if a drop of lime falls into that goblet, the milk will curdle. The cosmos is trying to teach us how careful we need to be on this path. That one drop can change the very essence of what you want to offer.

We go on living as though this is it, although we know that all this is temporary. The permanent stuff is on a larger level, neglected or shoved under the rug. We believe in God, life after death, reincarnation and karma, but we live in a manner that this life is it. We know that in the blink of an eye, destiny and intentions can change, but we go about with eyes shut.

Pure intent if not backed by noble action is similar
to a strategically placed well, filled with sludge
and murky water.

The day we realize that everything and everybody, including oneself, is a work in progress, one begins to be less judgemental and full of Oneness.

When a thought comes to you, you have the power to delete, store or encourage. If the thought is not about one's overall well-being, ideally, one should delete it, and if you cannot, then make sure you neither encourage it nor fight it.

Heaven and hell are not real-estate destinations. They exist within us. To become truly free, one needs to live each moment, without seeking heaven or judging the inhabitants of hell.

Sometimes, a glass of cool water is far more desired than even moksha. Each moment has its own demands. Often, nothing is wrong or right, but the timing of it.

The hour before dawn is the darkest but also the most spiritual—the true meditative Kali; you either fear the darkness or go within and become one with Her radiance.

Darkness has power only in the absence of light. But all the darkness in the world can't overpower a humble, lit matchstick.

The real journey begins when one cannot bear the darkness of one's own soul. The search for light commences only then.

Don't flog yourself. You'll achieve nothing but remorse and regret. Correct what you can. Accept what you have to. Strive to spread the light in every and any way you can.

Fear cannot touch those who know that The Divine can
never be wrong and never be unjust.

On the one hand there is karma. Then the play of planets. Then our inclinations. Then our free will. Then our stupidities. On the other hand is complete, positive surrender that you know best. How hard can it be to decide?

VI

Gratitude

No matter what, always know you are blessed.

To be able to enjoy what one has is a gift. To be able to forget or let go of pain, angst or what one will never have is sheer grace.

A glow-worm can never grasp the vastness of the sun.
All it needs to do is happily glow.

Humility comes forth from certainty, that all good that flows from each one of us is only and solely because of Grace.

If one has reasonable health, a semblance of family life, a roof to sleep under, food on the table, clothes to wear, and yet one is miserable, God help us if true misfortune pays a visit.

The path of gratitude is the true path. It's a painful path.
But it is the only path where our love is not only truly
tested but weighed, measured and clothed, not by
The One but by our own self.

It's strange—the darker the room, the more brilliant the flame that shines forth. Sometimes, one has to be bathed with the cold strife of discomfort to appreciate the warmth of normalcy.

One is content with one's lot; however simple this may sound, it is one of the pillars of spirituality and the cornerstone of happiness.

I would like to believe that to live in a state of humility, filled with compassion and joyous gratitude, are the foundations of spirituality.

To be able to enjoy what one has or earns, however meagre or immense, is a blessing.

If one decides to find flaws in everything, then even heaven will be left wanting and if one decides to accept all in gratitude, even hell will be a profound learning experience.

Sometimes, one's entire philosophy, life and spirituality, can be summed up in one's attitude of whether the glass is half empty or half full. The former indicates playing the victim and perpetual discontent, while the latter is in a state of gratitude.

Even the loftiest of eagles have to swoop down for sustenance and thus survive. The wise are aware of this and always have their head held high, but with feet firmly on the ground.

Ill-health cripples not only the body but often the heart, mind and the very essence of the individual. It makes many bitter and fragile. Only those immersed in gratitude come out unscathed.

Only those who have gone through turbulence, shocks, disasters and insecurities can appreciate the importance of normal, nothing-truly-happening day-to-day life.

Only those who have accepted their lot with calm and even joyous surrender to the divinity of the laws of karma, and continue to give their best to the moment, experience true freedom and liberation.

VII

Love and Relationships

We have countless roles to play. We are a child of
someone, a parent to our kids, a spouse, a lover, a friend,
a sibling, a teacher, a student, an employer, an employee,
and citizens of the world. Spirituality shines forth
the greatest when we can play each role with the only
intention of spreading happiness, love, and come forth
with compassion.

To love and being in love are two different species.
In the first, there is give and take involved; in the other,
one can't help but just love no matter what.

If you want unconditional love, then become a disciple. If you want to love unconditionally, then become a Master.

True love only gives, never seeks.

The more advanced the phone gets, our communication seems to be having less and less of substance.

We sometimes forget that the most important thing in our quest for spirituality is to spread love and joy within and around us, and give our best to life and then leave the rest to The One.

Trust is the perception we have of somebody. When the person moves away from that perception, we feel betrayed. We feel our trust has been broken. Acceptance is the love we have for an individual. You can't be betrayed when you come from acceptance.

To love truly means to love unconditionally.
All else is business.

Love always hopes for the best for one's lot and when failure comes forth, love provides the shade from harsh reality. Love never seeks for itself, it only gives.

Don't love somebody so much that he or she can't breathe. Love is made up of all elements, including the element of space.

Do I love thee for what you can do for me or do I love thee because I love only thee? But would I love thee if you could do nothing for me is a thought that questions my very sanity.

We are together as a family most often because we have serious karma to exchange. Or, one has come down to help the other to move spiritually higher at a faster pace. It's certainly not to accumulate more karma or get sucked into the karmic blueprint of the other. It is to assist. To grow. To teach. To learn. To carry but still strengthen. It is all and yet more but certainly not to destroy one's spiritual growth, worrying or pacifying or justifying.

When you love somebody truly, each moment of the day
is passed in the thought of your loved one or lover. If God
was the beloved, then each moment, no matter what you
did, you would go about in His or Her thought.

Once you are already engrossed and contained by Him or Her, then would there be a need to sit and pray, or go on a pilgrimage when your beloved resides within you?

Souls who grow up as friends and keep the bond of
friendship throughout life are the ones who are karmically
linked with each other. As they could not get a berth
on God's train of a family relationship, they chose to be
friends with a link that no power on earth can separate;
the force that binds them together comes from the power
of God and when His/Her hands hold the bond, it can
never, never be separated.

It makes sense to hate and love for the right reasons. But who has the time for all this? We hate for a lark and love at a whim and thus war and lawyers reign.

Why is it that when we become different we have grown and when others behave otherwise, they have changed?

Respect can vanish in a second. Love can wither in a moment. But a relationship based on accepting the good and the not-so good has a chance of permanence. That's why a dog is man's best friend and not the other way round.

In this battle of the good versus the nuisance, if we are filled with radiance due to the devices of those who want to harm us, then our very detractors and enemies have helped us climb the mountain higher, nudged us to shine brighter, made us see clearer. Then how can they be not our greatest well-wishers?

VIII

Compassion

The fragrance that you spread around with your love and compassion to fellow human beings is the work of God.

There is a certain grace in giving silently, which only those who come with true humility know about. *Baki sab tamasha hain.* (The rest is a show.)

There is a very thin line between philanthropy and self-gratification. But how does that matter? Just keep giving.

A simple act of giving makes The One and all the Masters and the Angels so happy. So, there must be something very profound, something very spiritual and something very pure in the act of giving. You have the heaven applauding and showering blessings and prayers on the giver.

Being compassionate and noble does not mean lying down and letting others walk over you. Don't confuse spirituality with weakness or stupidity.

To be able to feed the hungry, to clothe the naked, to heal the ill, to help those down and out are something each of us can do every now and then without stress. Imagine if all the haves become compassionate; then how can have-nots exist?

Our appreciation or encouragement of somebody might change the person's life. Imagine the power of words. It can create and it can destroy. Such power needs to be led by a very compassionate heart.

When an individual, with a true heart, forgives or blesses somebody, the dirt of earlier experiences clinging to the aura gets cleansed and it does not carry the past hurt, angst and the need for justice. Once that happens, both the people, who may have some *lena–dena*, or give and take, with each other, are freed from that experience. Thus, one is freed from some unpleasant experience due to a generous act of selflessness.

In charity, you give. In compassion, you share. When you give, you have to receive the same from the same individual. When you share, it spreads a bond of giving which goes on for lifetimes, with or without you.

Being honest is commendable, but being able to convey the truth with compassion is a gift. Like salt, too much or too little, can mess up the greatest of meals.

Brilliance, wit, courage, largeness of heart, genius, looks, character and even spirituality are all hollow if not accompanied by compassion, humility, and living in a state of calm surrender.

It takes a lot of courage to forgive. It's not for the faint-hearted. You need a large heart and a very small ego.

Only a tree on the side of a road knows the importance of the morning dew. Sometimes, a little help to those in need can make an unimaginable difference. Thus, always give no matter how little it may seem.

Failure that makes one a more compassionate human being is far greater than success, which makes the individual full of himself or herself.

Charity and extending compassion are two different animals. I have seen people refuse with such humility that it softens the heart, and have seen people give in a manner that shrivels the soul.

If we cannot forgive, what right do we have to seek forgiveness from Him up there? Logic demands that if you believe in an eye for an eye, then be ready to lose an eye, or worse, your spiritual wisdom.

I feel sometimes the cosmos has no other way to make
us more compassionate than by making us experience
hunger, pain, sorrow, loss and anguish. The wise learn
from these experiences and become more understanding.
Others waste the opportunity and become negative.
Karma means going through an experience, while free will
decides heaven, hell or in-between.

Do you know what the greatest miracle is? Leading an individual from darkness towards light is the greatest miracle, as everything noble and good begins when an individual starts embracing the Divine Light and walks on the path of radiance.

When we uplift somebody who is without hope, either
through word, action or assistance, we make the heaven
glow brighter and spiritual scriptures worth their wisdom.
Pain opens the door to compassion and love for all of
creation, and this unlocks the door to paradise and
God consciousness.

IX

Energy

Energy has no emotion. Like water, it takes the shape of whatever intent we harbour it with. The wise ones try to contain it with spirituality, the others with physicality.

Nature is raw energy. It is double-edged and gives and takes without emotion. We are all aware of the importance of fire and the devastation it can wreak. The five elements can bring heaven and hell into our lives. We are five elemental. We too thus can create heaven and hell within ourselves.

The true role of any individual is to allow the unhindered and uncorrupted Divine Energy to flow through him or her. That, in reality, is our only purpose of existence.

Like the rays of the sun that never discriminate, the energy of The Master is for all; how the energy is received, whether the doors are shut or curtains are put up to ward off the rays, that depends on each individual.

We all have to go through incarnating, like any other living species, and sometimes, we carry with us the lower energies of a particular species. This is part of our spiritual and karmic growth through various lifetimes, till even as a human being we continue to harbour and nurture that particular lower tendency or energy.

The lower energies want to make you a vehicle to create disharmony and madness, as that is their food and subsistence. They are present everywhere as the doors of paradise are shut to such energies and they roam about the fringes of creation feeding off the uncentredness of all living beings.

X

Calmness

When you really look at things with a calm mind,
which means with a calm aura, you realize the futility
of most actions and desires.

We need to work out the time when body, soul and spirit are in the greatest harmony and then go ahead and maintain that schedule which we should be able to keep up for the rest of our lives.

Reaction of any kind is going to only make matters worse. Being calm is not only the right thing to do spiritually, but also the most intelligent and practical way to embrace the moment.

The wonderment of being content and in serene acceptance of each moment is a blessing even the heaven aspires for.

So fragile is our state of mind that a single thought, word, glance can rattle one's sanity or well-being, thus focus more on the spirit within, than the mind.

All of heaven and beyond reposes in the womb
of calm silence.

When I am tired, I sometimes shut my eyes and imagine
I am nothingness—in these moments I feel refreshed.
When one is full of oneself and the world, it's a relief
to become nothingness. No ego . . . no world.
No world . . . no ego.

Our priorities—spiritual, emotional, intellectual, financial and social—need to be in harmony with each other. That and only that can lead us to our destination and eventual salvation.

When we sit silently or be within calmly, initially there
will be more chaos. Like steam rising from the scorched
earth when the rain falls. But as the rain continues, the
fragrance of mother earth envelops us. Silence is that
fragrance. Just keep at it and the *khushboo* of silence
will intoxicate. It has to.

The space of time between inhalation and exhalation
is most important. Sages claim that when this space
increases, the state of samadhi reigns.
It's all about space.

Youth need not always mean joy and vitality just as
old age need not translate into wisdom and maturity.
Eventually, everything is what each strives for—a state of
mind and receptiveness.

There is something divine about the radiance of the fire, the sound of the waves on a calm sea, the gentle rain, cool breeze, the majesty of mountains, flowing meadows, open space and a content human being.

The breath determines one's thoughts. Thoughts influence our words. The breath, thoughts and words become fuel for our deeds. Thus, it all originates from breath, and leads to deeds that eventually germinate into karma which becomes all pervasive as one's destiny and karmic blueprint. You do not become what you eat, you become what you think.

To go within is most important but it isn't possible
without calmness, and calmness isn't possible without
true surrender that you know best; so be it.

Dawn and twilight look the same. Dawn the promise
of sunbreak. Twilight the absence of radiance. In a
calm heart, one beckons hope and the other rest. In an
unsettled mind, fear and void.

Peace is a state of mind. Bliss is a state of being.

When you come from calmness, peace and well-being to all, compassion and forgiveness, then you use your free will to liberate yourself and also those who are knotted up with you in the karmic dance of give and take.

As Baba often says till life's motto becomes 'I shall not react, but calmly act', nothing's going to give.

Let meditation be the food, the sweets, the chocolates, the purest of the pure food for your physical bodies, and the proof of the pudding will be in the serenity, in the silent mind which you will create again from the trash of life.

When calm, nothing matters, and when restless, even heaven would leave one disgruntled. I guess that is why there are earthbound souls.

Don't ask for miracles. Make yourself the miracle of acceptance, joy, courage and calmness.

Focus on breath and you automatically focus on God.

Being in the moment is being in the present and that is virtually being in tune with The Creator who is presence and present personified.

Enlightenment is a state of mind. Oneness is a state of being.

Keep calm. Be joyful. Our greatest test is to go beyond the mind, the thoughts, the logic, the injustice, and just have faith in the wisdom, grace and compassion of The One.

XI

Karma

The fastest way to surrender and grow and burn away all karma is to get consumed by the fire of the love for one's Master. No gyan or philosophies. No meditation. No prayers. Nothing is needed. Just selfless love and absolute surrender.

When the karmic balance sheet is reworked, we are not present to justify our thoughts, words or deeds. Karma has no emotion, no logic, just the law of cause and effect.

No matter how much one may love another, the final walk is always done alone . . . carrying one's karma, if truly deserving, then with one's Master.

Karma is so often a byproduct of seeing, hearing and observing evil and doing nothing about it. Krishna went hoarse trying to explain to us that doing evil and being a mere observer of evil will be judged on the same weighing scale.

No matter how wrong somebody is, the moment we judge or slander, we have begun a karmic account with that individual wherein the karmic ledger we owe that person and the karmic debt is a heavy cross to carry.

Often, karma is nothing but action, thought, word or intent, created due to ignorance and selfishness.

When the ramification of karma or stupidity is inevitable, seek strength and wisdom and lots of humour to go through whatever is in store for us, and do it with grace and laughter.

The impact of karmic milestones which have to be mandatorily experienced can be controlled, and the magnitude and intensity can be tapered down via prayers and calmness and compassion for all of creation, including oneself.

The more we gravitate towards the external, the more karma is created, and once karma comes into play, for lifetimes we get sucked into this never-ending mire of sinking sand.

Every day is a new day in the realm of spirituality and to The One keeping the karmic balance sheet. Howsoever murky the accounts, we have a chance to redeem ourselves bit by bit, and no matter how glowing the deeds, we need to be constantly on guard, as sometimes one wrong word can push us back by lifetimes.

Why would anybody believe in the laws of karma and reincarnation and still lead a life filled with dark desires and conduct is something that goes against common sense and logic. But we still lead a life which suggests that there is no law of cause and effect, and afterlife is a myth. As species, mankind has left the very heavens confounded and dizzy.

When rough times hit with all the planetary force, very few remain the same thence. One can either become bitter, angry, negative, or calm, humble and compassionate. Karma decides the playing field. Free will decides how we play.

Every grape has the potential of being a great wine and every caterpillar doesn't become a butterfly. Eventually, one needs grace and this comes about when annihilation of one's ego takes place. When there is no self, there can be no karma. More self, more karma. No self, no karma.

Life is most often unpalatable. The meals dished out in the karmic kitchen taste like crap. That doesn't mean one has to cut off one's tongue. You just never know. The most sublime delicacy might be waiting for you just a spoonful away.

One cannot stop a raging fire by tackling it with more fire. Karmic fire can only be doused by calmness and inner strength. Not aggression and in a reactive manner.

God isn't involved in our free will or karma.
That is our responsibility.

The easiest way to work out one's karma, clean the slate of karmic dues and protect oneself and one's family, is through prayers, charity, meditation and positive acceptance.

I wonder if we are going to remember our bank balance or the position of power or one's looks or strength. I am sure we are going to wonder if there is a life after this body is dropped; if one has lived a life worthy of the next; if the next life is going to be miserable due to the ramifications of our free will and the hurt one has caused; and if only there was a little more time, one would have spread more happiness amongst one's lot.

Knowing something and using that knowledge appropriately and with humility is not one and the same thing. We all know about karma and that we are going to be as dead as rusted lamp posts, but we go about life as though this is the be-all and end-all of our journey.

XII

Devotion

The heaven above understands best the language of intention and devotion.

Every conqueror becomes like a mist in the ocean in time to come. Blessings are eternal. The warriors of light focus on permanence. Conquerors come and go.

Be it preparing a breakfast for the family or cleaning the toilet seat, if it's done as an offering to one's God and Master, then the individual is in perpetual *seva*, or service, to The Master, and then like a lotus one is in the world but not of it.

The more one focuses on The Path, the greater the distractions and negativity one attracts. In a way, it's as though all of the dark forces want you to fail. Only when one operates with humility, calmness and childlike faith, can one swim upstream. Of course, there are innumerable hurdles against the current expeditions. Just keep at it.

The foundation of perpetual growth is not based on talent or genius but on dedication, perseverance and, most importantly, calm, positive surrender.

Know oneself. The easiest way out is with brutal honesty, list down the strengths, weaknesses and limitations of one's self. Once we know what we are made of and then plan our journey onwards, it shall proceed with fewer roadblocks. Focus and capitalize on our strengths, stay away or work on our weaknesses, and try to overcome one's limitations.

XIII

Oneness

No matter how insignificant our lives or our own self-worth may seem, the fact is, within us there is life, and life emanates from The Creator, and thus, within us resides The One, and thus, each one of us is truly significant.

Every card player is aware that most often, it's not what cards one has been dealt with, it's what we do with the cards in hand that matters.

When an individual has the potential and is not moving towards his or her objective, that is one of the greatest tragedies of creation. It is like the cosmos has invested a particular energy, and you and I are wasting it away.

All is not destined. Most of it may be, but each individual has a certain part of life where free will rules. The higher you grow spiritually, the greater the free will you will have in your grasp.

God resides in each one. You need to dive within to reach The Pearl.

The only way one can live with dignity is when one truly respects all beings, including oneself.

The desire to be loved and praised is one of the greatest obstacles in being true to The One and ourselves. Never walk the line drawn by somebody else. Dance to your rhythm. Be cool.

Does a lotus lose its essence when placed in a café instead of a temple? When we remain true to ourselves whether in a place of worship, casino, palace, hut, with sages or crooks, I believe that is being true to The One and to one's own self.

If you and I are created by The One, then we imbibe within us The One. It may be in a very dormant or miniaturized state and not in that same dynamic magnitude, but each one of us has to have within us all that The Creator embodies or the same Divine Presence.

You are in charge and you will decide when to encourage and when to delete and when to store each thought or emotional impulse that comes within your orbit. You have to make it clear to your mind, heart, body, that you are in charge. If you do not, then there is chaos.

When elephants walk, dogs bark. How silly would it be for an elephant to change its route in order to avoid the cacophony of a few animals? Stay firm on your path. Haters will hate. Just walk on, friend.

The Divine Flame that burns within each of us has the power to light up the cosmos, but we still roam about in circles in the dark.

The more I observe mankind, the more I realize that for every rotten apple, there are orchards of fresh fruit waiting to spread their fragrance and nourishment.

In spirituality, nothing is of more paramount importance than being true to oneself. Honesty towards oneself is crucial if we want to walk this path.

For whatever reason, right or wrong, we can hoodwink the world but for god's sake, never try to mislead oneself. We might get away with the former. The latter will only lead to depression, void, frustration; you might be covered in glory but within, there shall be only emptiness.

The truth of life is that in each being exists The One.